The Hound of the Baskervilles
By Sir A. Conan Doyle

Director's Edition
(Reader's Edition also available.)

ISBN: 978-1-312-08013-3

Adapted for performance as part of the Living Literature program for the University of Minnesota – Duluth School of Fine Arts and Glensheen, the Historic Congdon Estate;

This script is intended for staged reading, and can be freely used for that purpose. Sound effects, scoring, and additional considerations can be provided by contacting
Dr. Rob Larson:
Robert.larson@egs.edu

Cast of Characters
4 M, 2 F

Sherlock Holmes (male)
Dr. Watson (male)
Stapleton (male)
Miss Stapleton (female)
Sir Henry Baskerville (male)
Mrs. Laura Lyons (female)

PROLOGUE (an old letter read by Holmes or Sir Henry)

I, William Baskerville, write this for my sons in the year 1742. My father told me about the Hound of the Baskervilles, and I believe his story was true. I want you, my sons, to read this story carefully. I want you to know that God punishes those who do evil, But never forget that He will forgive those who are sorry for any evil they have done.

A hundred years ago, in 1640, the head of the Baskerville family was Sir Hugo Baskerville. He was a wild and evil man. He was cruel and enjoyed hurting people. Sir Hugo fell in love with the daughter of a farmer who was a neighbor of his. The young woman was afraid of the evil Hugo, and avoided him. One day, Hugo heard that her father and brothers were away. He knew that she would be alone. So he rode to the farm with five or six of his evil friends. They made the girl go back to Baskerville Hall with them, and locked her in a room upstairs.

As usual, they drank bottle after bottle and soon they began to sing and laugh and shout evil words. The girl upstairs, who was already very frightened, felt desperate when she heard the terrible things they were shouting. So she did a very brave thing. She opened the window, climbed out of the room and down the ivy on the wall. Then she started to run across the moor towards her home.

A little while later, when he found an open window and an empty room, he screamed that he would give himself to the Devil if he caught the girl before she reached home. He ran from the house and unlocked his dogs. Then he jumped on to his black horse, and rode off over the moor with the hounds running and crying around him.

Hugo's friends fetched their horses and followed until, at last, they caught up with the hounds.

Standing at the head of a deep valley, they found the hounds, with their ears and tails down, very frightened. On the flat ground ahead, lay the girl. She had fallen there, dead of fear and exhaustion. Sir Hugo's body was lying near her.

But it was not the sight of Sir Hugo or the girl that so filled the men with fear. It was the sight of the huge animal standing over Sir Hugo. Its teeth were at his throat. It was a great black creature that looked like a hound. But it was larger than any hound they had ever seen.

As they watched, it tore out Hugo Baskerville's throat. Then it turned towards them. Its eyes were burning brightly. Its body shone with a strange light. Blood ran from its mouth. The men screamed and kicked their horses. They rode away as fast as they could…that night one of the men died from the horror he had seen. The others were mad for the rest of their lives.

That was the first time the Hound appeared, my sons. It has been seen many times since then, and many of the Baskervilles have died in strange and terrible ways. Because of this I warn you not to cross the moors at night. The Devil finds it easy to do his work when the world is dark.

SCENE I

Watson (narrator)
I had spent the brightest part of the day aboard a train, as London and its countryside was enjoying a beautiful late spring. I had enjoyed a pleasant luncheon, and was reading the newspaper. As I read, the words of an incredible letter ran through my mind, adding to the mystery at hand. I was about to meet Sir Henry Baskerville, sole heir to the Baskerville Hall in Devonshire. Sir Charles Baskerville, Henry's Uncle, died suddenly three months ago. His death caused much excitement in Devonshire among the townspeople and in the news. Sir Charles was a sensible man, but he believed the story sensationalized in the daily mail. And now his Nephew, convinced something terrible will happen in the next twenty-four hours, begs for the help of Sherlock Holmes.

Holmes, bored with the entire matter, sends me instead.

(END OF SCENE I – AUDIENCE MOVES)
SCENE II

Watson (narrating)
Arriving on schedule in Devonshire, Baskerville Hall was already visible in the distance. As I made my way on foot, I was met by a man I did not know.

Stapleton
'I hope you will excuse me for introducing myself, Dr Watson. My name is Stapleton. May I walk along with you? You are on the way to meet Sir Henry? This path to the Hall goes near my home, Pen House. Please come along with me and meet my sister.'

Watson (Narrating)
I accepted Stapleton's invitation, and we walked together.

Stapleton
'I know that you are a close friend of Sherlock Holmes...Has Mr Holmes any ideas about Sir Charles' death?'

Watson
'I'm afraid I can't answer that question,

Stapleton
'Will Mr Holmes visit us himself?'

Watson
'He can't leave London at the moment.

Watson (narrating)
I was rather surprised that he was asking me these questions. We walked on. As we did so, Stapleton told me that he and his sister had lived in

Devonshire for only two years. They had moved there soon after Sir Charles had begun to live in Baskerville Hall. He also talked about the moor and how it interested him. He told me to look across the moor to a place which was a bright green colour.

Stapleton
'That is the Great Grimpen Marsh...If animals or men go into the marsh, they will sink into it and die. But I can find my way to the very centre of it. It is an evil place, the Great Grimpen Marsh.'

Watson
'But you say you can go safely in and out of it?

Stapleton
'Yes, there are a few paths, and I have found them. That is where I can find the unusual plants and butterflies. I collect them.

Watson
'I shall try my luck one day.

Stapleton
'Please don't try. You would never return alive, and it would be my fault.'

SOUND EFFECT
(A long, low cry, very deep and very sad, comes over the moor. It fills the whole air and dies out)

Watson
What on Earth is that?

Stapleton
That is the sound...uhh...The people say it's the Hound of the Baskervilles, Sir. The Evil Hound which is calling for something to hunt and kill. I've heard many speak of it, but I have never heard it myself. Until now.

Watson
'You are a man of science. You don't believe that, do you? Isn't there a natural explanation for the sound?'

Stapleton
'A marsh makes strange noises sometimes. Perhaps it is the water and the wet ground moving.'

Watson
'But that was the voice of a living creature.

Stapleton
'Well, there are some very unusual birds on the moors. It was most probably the cry of one of those.'

Watson
Do you believe the story of the Hound?

Stapleton
As you say, I am a man of science. I have always believed that there are sensible explanations for everything. But....Sir Charles was a very worried man. He was near to breaking down. *He* believed this story of the Hound of the Baskervilles. *He* refused to go out at night.

Watson
How do you know for sure?

Stapleton
I remember driving up to the Hall one evening about three weeks before he died. He was standing at the door. I went up to him, and saw him staring at something behind me. There was a look of horror on his face. I turned quickly and saw something moving between the trees. It looked like a small black cow. He was so frightened. I stayed with him all the evening.

Watson (narrating)
At that moment a small butterfly flew across the path in front of us.

Stapleton
'Excuse me, Dr Watson!'

Watson (narrating)
He ran quickly and followed the butterfly on to the marsh, but he knew exactly where he could go, and was not in any danger. As I watched him, I heard the sound of steps behind me. I turned and saw a woman near me on the path. I was sure she was Miss Stapleton. She was very beautiful. Well dressed, with a lovely face. Before I could say anything, she said:

Miss Stapleton
'Go back! Go straight back to London, immediately. I cannot tell you why, but please do what I ask you, and never come near the moor again. But my brother is coming. Not a word to him.'

Watson (narrating)
Stapleton had caught the butterfly, and was walking back to us.

Stapleton
'Hello, my dear. (his voice was not completely friendly) 'I see that you two have already introduced yourselves.'

Miss Stapleton
'Yes, I was telling Sir Henry that it was rather late in the year for him to see the true beauty of the moor.'

Watson
'I am sorry. You have made a mistake. I'm not Sir Henry. I am a friend who is visiting him, and my name is Dr Watson.'

Miss Stapleton
'I'm sorry. Please forget what I said.

(a beat)
Stapleton
You may think this a lonely, strange place to live, but the moors are very interesting, and we enjoy it here. I owned a school in the north of England, but I had to close it. I miss the boys and girls, but there is plenty to do here, and we have good neighbours. I hope Sir Henry will become one of them. May I visit the Hall this afternoon to meet him, do you think?'

Watson
'I'm sure he will be very pleased to meet you. I must go on to the Hall now, and I shall tell him immediately.'

Watson (narrating)
I said goodbye to the Stapletons, and continued on the path back to the Hall.

(The audience is brought a little further along the path)

Watson (narrating)
I had been walking for only a few minutes when I was surprised to see Miss Stapleton sitting on a rock ahead of me. She was breathing quickly, and I realized she had run by a quicker way to get ahead of me.

Miss Stapleton
'Dr Watson, I want to say sorry for the mistake I made. I thought you were Sir Henry. Please forget what I said. I did not mean you were in danger. Now I must go, or my brother will miss me.'

Watson
'I cannot forget your words, Miss Stapleton. 'If Sir Henry is in danger, I must tell him.'

Miss Stapleton
'You know the story of the Hound?'

Watson
'Yes, but I do not believe it…

Miss Stapleton
'But I think it's true. Please persuade Sir Henry to leave this place. So many of his family have died here mysteriously. He must not put his life in danger by staying here.'

Watson
'Sir Henry won't leave this place without a real reason.

Miss Stapleton
'I can't give you a real reason. I don't know anything for certain.'

Watson
'One more question, Miss Stapleton. 'The story of the Hound is well known. Why didn't you want your brother to hear what you said?'

Miss Stapleton
'My brother wants the head of the Baskerville family to live in the Hall. He wants Sir Henry to continue the good work that Sir Charles began. He doesn't want Sir Henry to go and live in another place. So he doesn't want me to talk about the Hound. I must go now, or my brother will guess I have been speaking to you. Good-bye!'

Watson (narrating)
She turned and went back towards her house, and I walked on to Baskerville Hall.

(End of SCENE II)
SCENE III

Watson
Upon arriving safely at the gate of the Great Hall of Baskerville, I had another sudden and unexpected greeting.

(Holmes pops out of the bushes, lively and perhaps over-caffeinated)

Holmes
The Butler, Barrymore, said one thing in his report that was certainly not true.

Watson
Holmes! Good Heavens! But I thought you were—

Holmes
I needed you to think that. It was critical to the case.

Watson
But—

Holmes
The Butler said that there were no other prints on the ground around the body. He did not notice any. But I did. (pointing) Not close to the body, but they are fresh and clear.'

Watson
'Footprints?
Holmes
'Yes. Footprints.

Watson
'A man's or a woman's?

Holmes
Neither. They are the footprints of a huge hound!'

(Holmes yawns.)

Watson
I see.

Holmes
(directing with his hands the scene as he goes)
On the night of his death, Sir Charles Baskerville went out for his walk to think and to smoke his usual cigar. He was going to London on the next day, his butler was packing his suitcases. (pointing out a particular spot) The Butler said Sir Charles seems to have stood here for five or ten minutes…we know that because his cigar had burned down and the ash had dropped twice off the end of it.

Watson
The Butler observed this?

Holmes
Quite right. This Butler is a very good detective, Watson. He saw Sir Charles' prints and ash, though he missed the houndprints.

Watson
Hmm.

Holmes
By midnight the Butler worried that Sir Charles had not returned, so he went to look for him. He found (this) door of the Hall open. The day had been rainy and wet so Barrymore saw the prints left by Sir Charles' shoes as he had walked down the Alley. Half-way down the Alley, the ashes, signs that Sir Charles had stood there for some time. Barrymore followed the footprints to the far end of the Alley. And there he found Sir Charles' body.

Watson
Anything else?

Holmes
Barrymore reported something interesting about the footprints. He said that they changed as he followed them from the ashes. They changed from whole footprints to toe prints.

Watson
Toe Prints?

Holmes
Yes, as though Sir Charles had walked on his toes.

(Sir Henry opens the doors and calls from the Baskerville Estate entrance.)

Henry
Holmes and Watson, I presume? Come in! Come in!

(End of Scene III – Audience moves inside)
SCENE IV

Sir Henry
Several people have seen an animal on the moor that looks like an enormous hound. They all agree that it was a huge creature, which shone with a strange light like a ghost. I have questioned these people carefully. They are all sensible people. They all tell the same story. Although they have only seen the creature far away, it is exactly like the hell-hound of the Baskervilles' story. The people are very frightened, and only the bravest man will cross the moor at night.'

Holmes
Do you, Sir Henry, believe that the creature is supernatural - something from another world?

Henry
I don't know what to believe.

Watson
'But you must agree that the footprints were made by a living creature, not a ghost?'

Henry
'When the hound first appeared two hundred and fifty years ago, it was real enough to tear out Sir Hugo's throat...but it was a supernatural hell-hound.

Holmes
Look, if you think that Sir Charles' death was caused by something supernatural, my detective work can't help you.'

(Holmes acts like he will leave.)

Henry
You must understand my concern! So many Baskervilles who come here die horrible deaths! But Uncle Charles' good work must go on. If it doesn't, all the people on the Baskerville lands will be much poorer. If the Baskerville family leaves the Hall, that is what will happen. I don't know what to do. Tonight is my first night in the Hall. I've been confined to the Hotel.

Holmes
Hmm. And you did mention in your letter a strange note you received at the Hotel?

Henry
Yes. Just a moment.

(Henry goes to fetch it. After he is out of sight...)
Watson
'What do you think of this case?

Holmes
'It is hard to say. Take, for example, the change in the footprints. Did Sir Charles walk on his toes down the Alley? Only a stupid person is likely to believe that. The truth is he was running - running for his life. He ran until his heart stopped and he fell dead.
Watson
Running from what?

Holmes
Fear. (plainly) He didn't know what he was doing. That explains why he ran away from the house instead of towards it. He was running away from help. The next question: Who was he waiting for that night? And why was he waiting outside, and not in the house?'

Watson
'You think he was waiting for someone?'

Holmes
'Sir Charles was old and unwell. We can understand why he took a walk each evening. But why did he stand in the cold, on wet ground, for five or ten

minutes? The Butler cleverly noted the cigar ash, so we know how long Sir Charles stood there. We know that he was afraid, so it wasn't likely he stood around outside each evening.

(Henry enters with a note. He puts a piece of paper on the table. On it are the words: 'Do not go on to the moor. If you do, your life will be in danger.' The words had been cut out of a newspaper.)

Henry
Here it is. Can you tell me, Mr Holmes, what this means, and who is so interested in me?

Watson
(Reading) 'Do not go on to the moor. If you do, your life will be in danger.' The words are cut out of a newspaper.

Holmes
'This is very interesting,' (he holds it up in front of his face) 'Look how badly it has been done. I think the writer was in a hurry. Perhaps the writer was working out of the hotel…(He tosses the letter down, bored with it.) 'Now, Sir Henry, have you anything else to tell us?'

Henry
'No…

Holmes
All right. I bid you farewell.

Henry
(urgently) Except that I have lost another one of my shoes.

Holmes
(stopping) Is that right?

Henry
I put a pair outside my door last night. I wanted…the hotel…to clean them, but when I went to get them this morning, one had gone.

Holmes
One shoe seems a useless thing to steal…I am sure the shoe will be found in the hotel and returned to you. (Holmes continuing to exit)

Henry
But you see this is the second time it has happened! (Holmes stops) I had...purchased brand new shoes, and one of those had been taken. The second missing shoe was an old shoe. Who would want one old shoe?

Watson
Or one new shoe, for that matter.

Holmes
Hmm…curious…Well, let me ask you, in light of the present circumstances…is it sensible for you to be here at Baskerville Hall? There seems to be danger here for you.

Henry
There is no man or devil who will keep me from the home of my family.

Holmes
Good. What I know is this: Somebody is following you. If someone tries to harm you apart from here, it will be hard to stop him or catch him afterwards. Here, we have a better chance.' Now, are there any other persons presently tending to the estate?

Henry
Barrymore, the Butler. And his wife.

Holmes
'Did the Barrymores receive anything from Sir Charles' will? And did they know that they would get some money when he died?'

Henry
'Yes, They each received £500, and Sir Charles told everyone what he had written in his will.

Holmes
That's very interesting.

Henry
I hope you don't suspect everyone who got something from the will. A lot of people received a little money. He gave a lot of money to a number of hospitals. The rest all went to me… £740,000.'

Holmes
'I had no idea it was so much.'

Henry
The Baskerville lands are worth about one million pounds.

Holmes
'Dear me, A man could kill for that much.

Henry
Excuse me?

Holmes
(to Watson, pointing at Henry) If something happens to our young friend here, then who would get Baskerville Hall and all its lands?'

Henry
Well, I am the only son of Uncle Charles' younger brother. The youngest brother of the three, Roger, was a criminal. The police wanted him, so he had to leave England. They say he looked exactly like the family picture of old Sir Hugo, who first saw the Hound. He was the same kind of man, too. He went to South America, where he died of a fever. So, if I die, there is no heir.

Holmes
I see. Well, I agree you should stay. But I must go. Watson will keep watch here with you, and report to me at 221B.

Watson
I suppose—I—

Holmes
That is all.

(Henry and Watson regard each other awkwardly)

End of SCENE IV
SCENE V

The following scene is a short montage of glances and exchanges between the four characters.

Watson (narrating)
Holmes disappeared as quickly as he appeared. Mr Stapleton came to the Hall and met Sir Henry that same afternoon. As the days went by, Sir Henry became acquainted with Stapleton and his lovely sister. They took us one morning through the Moors to the place where the evil Sir Hugo and the Farmer's Daughter died. We had a few lunches at Pen House.

In a short time, I observed that Sir Henry clearly thought Miss Stapleton was very beautiful. His eyes followed her everywhere. He liked her very much, and I considered that she felt the same about him. He spoke about her again and again in our private conversations. From the first meeting, we met the Stapletons almost every day.

After a short time it was clear that Sir Henry had fallen deeply in love with the beautiful Miss Stapleton. At first I thought that Stapleton would be very pleased if his sister married Sir Henry. However, I soon realized that he did not want their friendship to grow into love.

He did everything he could to make sure that they were never alone. On one or two occasions they did manage to meet alone, but Stapleton followed them and was not pleased to see them together.

(The scene shifts to the windows to the left of the audience.)

Watson (narration cont'd)
One night I was woken by a noise at about two in the morning. I heard someone walking softly outside my door. I got up, opened the door and looked out. I saw Sir Henry moving carefully and quietly away from me. I followed him, as quietly as I could. He was standing at the window. He was holding a light in his hand and looking out on to the moor. He stood without moving for a few minutes and then he put out the light. I stealthily attempted to leave without being detected.

(Watson causes an awful commotion, alerting Sir Henry. He re-lights his light.)

Henry
'What are you doing here, Watson?'

Watson
I—I was about to ask you the same thing.
Henry
Nothing…It was just the window. I go round at night to see that they are closed, and this one wasn't shut.

Watson
'Come now, Sir. No lies. What are you doing with that light? You were holding it up to the window.'

Henry
I—I--

Watson
I think you were sending a message. Let's see if there's an answer from someone on the moor.

(Watson holds the light up to the window, and looks out into the darkness. Suddenly a light answers from the moor.)

Henry
That's quite enough.

Watson
'There it is…(the light patterns copy each other) The light on the moor answered by moving in the same way…Now, Henry, who is your friend on the moor? What's going on?' '

Henry
That's my business…I won't tell you.

Watson
I see.

Henry
It's not awful. I--

(Just as he spoke there came a strange cry from across the moor. It was the same cry as before.)

Henry (cont'd)
'What is that noise?'

Watson
'I've heard it before. Stapleton says it's the cry of a bird.

Henry
It is the cry of a hound! What do the local people say it is?

Watson
They say it is the cry of the Hound of the Baskervilles.

Henry
'Can there possibly be some truth in the story? Am I really in danger from such an evil thing?

Watson
Of course not. And with the windows secure, we will be fine in any case. (a beat) Well, I suppose I will say good night.

Henry
Watson, before you go...I do have new information about Uncle Charles.

Watson
Yes?

Henry
I know why he was waiting outside. He was going to meet a woman.

Watson
'Sir Charles was meeting a woman? Who was the woman?'

Henry
'I don't know her name, but it begins with 'L.L.'

Watson
How do you know this?

Henry
'Well, Sir Charles got a letter on the morning of the day he died. It was from Newtown, and the address was in a woman's writing. Barrymore was cleaning the fireplace in his study this afternoon, and found a letter. Most of it was burned, but the bottom of one page was not burned. (he produces it from his pocket)

Watson
(Reading) "Please, please, burn this letter, and be out at the gate by ten o'clock. L.L."

Henry
We don't know who L.L. is, but if you could find out, you might learn more about Sir Charles' death.

(Suddenly there is a commotion from the windows, followed by a light. Miss Stapleton enters.)
Miss Stapleton
(surprised by Watson) I—Dr. Watson—

Henry
(embarrassed) Miss Stapleton, I am so humiliated. Forgive me.

Watson
(understanding) It is my mistake entirely. Good evening, all.

Henry
Watson, you might sit with us for a late night cup of tea.

Watson
I—that would not be appropriate.

Miss Stapleton
What of this is appropriate?

Watson
(thoughtfully) Say, Miss Stapleton: I expect you know almost everybody living near here. 'Do you know a woman whose names begin with the letters L.L.?'

Miss Stapleton
(looks to Henry first, then) 'Yes, Mrs Laura Lyons. She lives in Newtown.'

Watson
'Who is she?'

Miss Stapleton
'She's Old Mr Frankland's daughter. Laura married a painter called Lyons who came to paint pictures of the moor. But he was cruel to her, and after a while he left her. Her father will not speak to her, because she married against his wishes. So her husband and her father have made her life very unhappy.

Watson
But how does she live?

Miss Stapleton
'Several people who knew her sad story have helped her. My...brother and Sir Charles gave her some money. I gave a little myself. She used the money to start a typewriting business.'

Watson
I would certainly like to meet Mrs. Lyons.

Henry
Straightaway. I'll arrange for it in the early morning.

Watson
Very good. Well, then.

(Awkwardness)

(End of SCENE V – Audience moves into study)
SCENE VI

Watson (narrating)
I met with Mrs. Laura Lyons the next morning in one of the many Baskerville Hall sitting rooms. She was a very pretty lady with red hair. I told her who I was, and that I had come to help the Baskervilles.

Laura
Sir Charles Baskerville helped me when I was poor and hungry. When I was in serious trouble, the men in my life were of no help to me.

Watson
'It is about Sir Charles that I have asked to see you. I want to know if you ever wrote to him and asked him to meet you.'

Laura
(angry, pale) 'What a question! What right have you to ask me about my private life? But the answer is "no".

Watson
'Surely you are not remembering clearly. I think you wrote to him on the day that he died. And your letter said: "Please, please, burn this letter, and be out at the gate by ten o'clock"

Laura
No.

Watson
No?

Laura
(in a low voice) 'I asked Sir Charles to tell nobody.'

Watson
'You must not think that Sir Charles spoke to anyone about you. He put the letter on the fire, but not all of it was burnt. Now, did you write that letter to him?'

Laura
'Yes. Why should I be ashamed of writing to him? I wanted him to help me. I learned that he was going to London early on the following day, so I asked him to meet me before he went. I could not go to the Hall earlier that day.'

Watson
'But why did you ask him to meet you outside, instead of in the house?'

Laura
'Do you think it would be sensible for a woman to go at that time of night into the house of an unmarried man?'

Watson (narrating)
Remembering the events of the prior evening, I momentarily lost focus.

Watson (back in the scene)
'Well, what happened when you arrived?'

Laura
'I didn't go!'

Watson
'Mrs Lyons!'

Laura
'I tell you I did not go. Something happened that stopped me from going. I can't tell you what it was.'

Watson
'Mrs Lyons,' I said. 'If you did not see Sir Charles, you must tell me why. If you do not, it will look very bad for you if I have to go to the police with this new piece of information about the letter.'

Laura
(after a beat) 'I see that I must tell you. Perhaps you know that I married a man who was very cruel to me. I hated him and I wanted to get a divorce. But a divorce is expensive, and I had no money. I thought that if Sir Charles heard my sad story, he would help me to get a divorce.'

Watson
‘Then why didn't you come to see Sir Charles?'

Laura
'Because I got help from someone else.'

Watson
'Why didn't you write to Sir Charles and tell him?'

Laura
'I was going to, but then I saw in the newspaper the next morning that he had died.'

Watson (narrating)
I asked Mrs Lyons a number of other questions, but she did not change her story, whatever I asked her. I was not sure that she had told me the whole truth.

Why had she nearly fainted when I had told her about the letter?

(Mrs. Lyons exits...Audience and Watson move to final seats.)

Over the following days my own leads in the case cooled. Meanwhile, word spread around town of a mysterious man living out on the Moor. There were hundreds of the old stone huts on the moor...they could be faintly seen from the higher windows of the Baskerville Hall.

Barrymore, the Butler told me of a young boy who takes bags of food out to the man. Barrymore believed the man was an escaped prisoner.

Stapleton taught me how to walk the paths out on the Moor, and I ventured out alone one afternoon to discover the man for myself. One of the many huts had a fresh path worn up to the door.

I took my revolver out of my pocket (he does this as he tells the story), and checked that it was ready to fire. I walked quickly and quietly up to the hut, and looked inside. The place was empty.

There were some blankets on a flat stone where the man slept. There had been a fire in one corner. There were some cooking pots, and the bag the boy had been carrying. Under the bag I saw a piece of paper with writing on it. Quickly, I picked up the paper and read what was written on it.

It said: 'Dr Watson has gone again to Newtown.'
I realized that the mysterious man had told someone to watch me, and this was a message from his spy. Was the man a dangerous enemy? I felt lost, useless to the Baskerville cause, and now concerned for my own safety as well.

(a beat)

Back in the great Hall, through the windows, the sun was low in the sky. Everything looked calm and peaceful in the golden evening light. But I did not feel peaceful or calm. I felt frightened, wondering about the mysterious man.

(we hear the sound of footsteps from the windows to the left of the audience...Watson draws his revolver...the foot steps get louder, closer, then stop...silence...then a few more loud steps...we see a figure in the shadows. Watson takes aim at the figure.)

Holmes (in the shadows)
'It's a lovely evening, my dear Watson. I really think you might enjoy it more out here.'

Watson
'Holmes!? Holmes!' (Holmes enters) I have never been so glad to see anyone in my life, nor so surprised.'

Holmes
'I am surprised, too. How did you find me?'

Watson
You're the man in the hut? Ha! I learned about the boy with the food.

Holmes
'I guess that you have questioned Mrs Laura Lyons. When we put together everything that each of us has discovered, I expect we shall know almost everything about this case.'

Watson
'But how did you get here? And what have you been doing? I thought you had to finish your case in London.'

Holmes
'That is what I wanted you to think.

Watson
'Then you have tricked me. Again! And have no confidence in me.

Holmes
'I am sorry if it seems I have tricked you, my dear Watson. I did not want our enemy to know I was here, but I wanted to be near enough to make sure that you and Sir Henry were safe. You are a kind person - too kind to leave me alone out here in bad weather. Our enemy would guess I was here if he saw you coming out with food, or with important news. You have been a very real help to me. Your letters with all their valuable information have been brought to me. You have done excellent work, and without you I would not have all the important details I needed.'

Watson (narrating)
Holmes' warm words of thanks made me feel much happier, and I saw that he was right.

Holmes
That's better. Now tell me about your visit to Mrs Laura Lyons.

Watson (narrating)
I told Holmes everything Mrs Lyons had said.

Holmes (humourously regarding Watson and the audience, momentarily breaking that 'fourth wall'...) 'This is all very important. It answers questions I have been unable to answer. Did you know that Mrs Lyons and Stapleton are very close friends? (Is Holmes now addressing the audience, too?) They often meet, and they write to each other. Perhaps I can use this information to turn Stapleton's wife against him.

Watson
'His wife? Who and where is she?'

Holmes (to everyone, quickly)
'The lady called Miss Stapleton, who pretends to be his sister, is really his wife!'

Watson
'Good heavens, Holmes! Are you sure? If she is his wife, why did Stapleton allow Sir Henry to fall in love with her?'

Holmes (continuing, on a roll now)
'Sir Henry hurt nobody except himself when he fell in love with her. Stapleton took care that Sir Henry did not make love to her.

Watson (knowing more than he should)
Well...perhaps not enough care...

Holmes
Scandalous. (amused) I repeat that the lady is his wife, and not his sister. They came here only two years ago, and before that he owned a school in the north of England. He told you that, and you told me

in your letter. I checked on the school, and found that the man who had owned it went away with his wife when the school closed. They changed their name, but the couple who were described to me were without doubt the Stapletons.'

Watson
'But why do they pretend to be brother and sister?'

Holmes
'Because Stapleton thought that she would be very much more useful to him if she appeared to be a free woman.'

Watson
'So he is our enemy! And the warning note to Sir Henry at the Hotel came from Miss Stapleton.'

Holmes
'Exactly.'

Watson
'But if Miss Stapleton is really his wife, why is he a close friend of Mrs Laura Lyons?'

Holmes
'Your excellent work has given us the answer to that question, Watson. Mrs Lyons was getting a divorce. So I believe she hoped to marry Stapleton. He told her that he was unmarried, and that he wanted to make her his wife. When she learns the truth, she may decide to help us.

Watson
'One last question, Holmes. What is Stapleton trying to do?'

Holmes (in a low voice)
'Murder, cold-blooded murder. That is what Stapleton is trying to do. Do not ask me for details. I am about to catch him in a trap. There is only one danger - that he will act before I am ready.

(As he finishes speaking, an awful scream - a long cry of pain and horror - breaks the silence of the moor.)

Watson (gun ready)
'Oh, my God. 'What is that?'

(More cries, and added to them, the Hound.)

Holmes
'The hound! Come, Watson, come! Great heavens! If we are too late...'

They Exit. From behind the windows, Watson narrates.

Watson (narrating)
From somewhere in front of us came one more hopeless scream. Then we heard quick footsteps on the path. After a few moments, Sir Henry appeared out of the fog and walked on in the clear moonlight.

Holmes
'Listen! Sir Henry! Get Ready! Look out! It's coming!

Watson (narrating)
Revolver ready, I looked at Holmes. He looked like a man who was going to win the most important game of his life. Then suddenly his eyes nearly jumped out of his head, and his mouth opened in frightened surprise. I looked away from him to see what his eyes were fixed on. When I saw the awful shape that was coming towards us out of the fog, my blood turned cold. The revolver nearly fell from my hands, and my whole body froze with fear.

(Cue The Hound)

I saw a hound, an enormous black hound. It was bigger than any dog I had ever seen. Fire came from its open mouth. Its eyes were burning. Flames covered its head and body. It was a more horrible sight than anyone could imagine - a hell-hound sent by the devil.

The huge, black, burning hound ran quickly and silently after Sir Henry. He watched helplessly as the terrible creature got closer to him. Our friend was near to death, and we were helpless with fear.

Then our fear for Sir Henry became greater than our terror. We fired our revolvers together. The creature gave a loud cry of pain, and we knew we had hit it. When we heard the cry of pain, our fears disappeared.

This was no supernatural hound. Our bullets could hurt it, and we could kill it. We ran after it as fast as we could.

I saw the creature jump at Sir Henry and throw him to the ground. Its teeth went for his throat. But the next moment Holmes had emptied his revolver into the hound's body. It gave a last deep cry, its teeth closed on the empty air, and it fell to the ground. I put my revolver to its head, but I did not need to fire. The hound was dead.

Sir Henry lay unconscious where he had fallen. Quickly we opened the neck of his shirt. Holmes had fired just in time, and the hound's teeth had not reached our friend's throat. We carried him back into the safety of the Baskerville Hall.

Holmes
Good Work, Sir Henry. Good work, in deed.

(Watson and Holmes enter with Henry and set him down in the room on the floor.)

Watson
I must give this man immediate medical attention.

Holmes
No, Watson. Let him lie there for awhile.

Watson
Good God, man! This man has just been through a Hell of an ordeal!

Holmes
I am more worried about you, my dear man.

Watson
'My God! What was it? What in heaven's name was it?'

Holmes
'It's dead, whatever it was. We've killed the family ghost for ever.'

(From the shadows, Stapleton enters.)

Stapleton
'Dr Watson, is that you? But, dear me, what's this? Somebody hurt? Not - don't tell me that it's our friend Sir Henry!'
(Stapleton goes to Henry to get a better look)
'Dear me! How terrible! How did he die?'

Holmes
'We think he broke his neck by falling over. He was out running in the dark.'

Stapleton
'I heard a cry, and that is why I came out. I was worried about Sir Henry,'

Holmes
'Why were you worried about Sir Henry?'

Stapleton
'Because I had invited him to my house. When he did not come I was surprised. Then, when I heard cries on the moor, I began to worry about him. I wonder -- did you hear anything else at all?'

Holmes
'No. 'Did you?'

Stapleton
'No.'

Holmes
'What do you mean, then?'

Stapleton
'Oh, you know the stories about the supernatural hound. I wondered if it had been here tonight.'

Watson
(playing along) 'We heard nothing of that kind.

Stapleton
'You think this poor man simply fell to his death?'

Watson
It was quite dark.

Stapleton
'Do you agree, Mr Sherlock Holmes?'

Holmes
'You're quick to guess who I am.

Stapleton
'We've been expecting you ever since Dr Watson arrived.'

Holmes
It appears Sir Henry is clumsy. It's a sad death, but it won't stop me from returning to London tomorrow.

Stapleton
'Before you return, will you be able to explain the mysteries that we've experienced here?'

Holmes
Mysteries....(Holmes looks up the the portrait of Sir Hugo)...Indeed. Watson, could you tell me which Baskerville that is?'

(All look up at the portrait.)

Watson
'That is Sir Hugo, the one who started all the trouble. He was the first to see the Hound.'

(Holmes looks hard at the picture, but says nothing more. After a moment, he grabs a chair and stands on it so that he may put his face closer to it.)

Holmes
'Is it like anyone you know?'

Watson
'Good heavens!' (Holmes and Watson both look slowly over to Stapleton)

Holmes
'Yes. There's not much doubt about it. Stapleton is a Baskerville. He looks like Sir Hugo, and he has the same evil character. Now I understand why he wanted to kill Sir Henry. I am sure we shall find that he will inherit the Baskerville lands. Stapleton! We've caught you like one of your butterflies, and we shall add you now to the Baker Street collection.'

(Stapleton makes a move to escape, but Watson aims his revolver at him.)

Watson
Not another step.

Stapleton
You're all mad.

Holmes (yelling offstage)
We're ready for you!

(Enter Mrs. Laura Lyons. Holmes greets her, shakes her hand.)

Holmes
'Dr Watson has told me everything, Mrs Lyons. We see Sir Charles' death as a case of murder. Both Stapleton and his wife are suspects.'

Laura (shocked)
'His wife!' He has no wife. He is not a married man.'

Holmes
'I have come here ready to prove that he is married, and the woman who calls herself his sister is really his wife.' (yelling again) Enter, my poor girl! (Holmes hands Mrs. Lyons a few papers and a picture he produces from his pocket.)

(Enter Miss Stapleton. She is bruised on her face and there are cuts along her arms. She looks awful. Holmes helps her to sit near the fallen sir Henry.)

Watson
My Dear Miss Stapleton! What has happened to you?

Holmes
This cruel devil Stapleton has beaten her. Tied her up. I had a devil of a time sneaking her over here through the Moor.

Miss Stapleton
Oh, Henry! Henry! Look what he has done to us!'

(Miss Stapleton stumbles toward Sir Henry, and looks as though she will faint. Holmes and Watson help her into a chair, tensions rise as Stapleton looks for his escape...)

Laura (regarding the papers and Miss Stapleton, she becomes angry and sad)
What have you done?!! (she grabs Watson's revolver and points it at Stapleton) I thought this man loved me, but he has lied to me. Ask me what you like, Mr Holmes, and I will tell you the truth. I never thought any harm would come to Sir Charles. He was a dear old gentleman who was very kind to me. I would do nothing to hurt him.'

Holmes
'I believe you, Mrs Lyons. Now, let me tell you what I think happened. You can tell me if I'm right or if I'm wrong. I think Stapleton told you to write the letter to Sir Charles and to ask him for help. He also told you to ask Sir Charles to meet you outside at the moor gate. Then, after you had sent the letter, Stapleton persuaded you not to meet Sir Charles after all.'

Laura (to Stapleton)
'You told me that you could not allow any other man to give me the money for my divorce! You said you were poor, but that you would give all your money to bring us together. (to Holmes) Then, after I heard about Sir Charles' death, he told me to say nothing about my letter and the meeting. He said I would be a suspect. (back to Stapleton) You frightened me into staying silent.'

Holmes
'Yes. But you wondered about him?'

Laura
'Yes, but since he has lied to me about marrying me, I will no longer keep his secrets.'

Holmes
'You are lucky that you have escaped him. You know too much. But you are safe now.'

Miss Stapleton
(coming around) My body is beaten, but he has hurt me more in other ways. While I thought he loved me, I accepted many things. But he doesn't love me. He has used me.'

Holmes
I am sure, young woman, you were very frightened of your cruel husband, and you suspected that he was responsible for Sir Charles' death. Perhaps now, that all your love and fear for this man have finally gone, you'll help us?

Stapleton
Don't breathe a word, woman.

Holmes
Perhaps you'll show us where he keeps the phosphorous paint?

Stapleton
I am warning you...

Holmes
You knew about the hound, but it was just now when you learned of Mrs Lyons that any love left for your husband has vanished.

Miss Stapleton
You beat me!! You tied me up!! Because I know where he kept the dog. The glowing paint. How he starves the dog.

Stapleton
You will never be a Lady.

Miss Stapleton
A Lady? Are you mad? (To Holmes) He says that when he inherits the Baskerville lands, I will love him again. He thinks I will keep silent if I become 'Lady Baskerville'. (To Stapleton) But you are wrong. I will never forgive you or love you again. And you will never enjoy the results of your crime.

Watson
Of course. After what we've seen tonight, we cannot be surprised that Sir Charles died of fright. It's not surprising the poor man screamed and ran away as

he did. The old story of the supernatural hound probably gave Stapleton the idea of using phosphorus.

Holmes
Very clever. I said it in London and I say it again, Watson. We have never had a more dangerous enemy than the one standing before us.

Watson
It makes sense to me now. The picture shows us clearly that Stapleton is indeed a Baskerville.

Holmes
The son of Roger Baskerville, who was Sir Charles' younger brother. Roger was a criminal who escaped from prison and ran away to South America. Everyone thought he had died unmarried, but that was not true. He had one son, also called Roger. (pacing around Stapleton) You married, came to England, started a school in the north. You discovered that you would inherit the Baskerville lands and fortune if Sir Charles and Sir Henry both died. So you moved in right next door. Hidden in plain sight.

Stapleton
Quite a story.

Holmes
You met Sir Charles, you knew he believed these supernatural stories, and that he had a weak heart. You used phosphorus to make a poor, starved animal shine like the hound in the story.

Watson
'He needed to get Sir Charles out of the Hall at night.'

Holmes
'This would be easy to do if his wife made Sir Charles fall in love with her. But, although he beat her, she refused to help him with his evil plan.'

Watson
'Then Stapleton met Laura Lyons. She wrote the letter to bring Sir Charles outside on that sad night.

Holmes
The hound, shining with phosphorus, chased Sir Charles down the alley. Sir Charles' terror was so great that his weak heart stopped, and he died, but the animal did not touch the dead body.'
You see how clever Stapleton was. Neither he nor the hound had touched Sir Charles so there was no sign of murder. The only two people who might suspect him -- his wife and Mrs Lyons -- could not be certain about what he had done. Anyway, neither of them would inform the police about him.'

Miss Stapleton (crouched near Sir Henry)
When Sir Henry had reached England, we went to London. He locked me up in that hotel. I knew that he had some evil plan, but I was too frightened to give Sir Henry a clear warning. Instead—

(Holmes pulls the newspaper letter out and places it on the table)

Holmes
You sent him the letter made of words cut from a newspaper. When I looked at it, I held it close to my eyes. I noticed a smell of perfume, so I guessed that a woman had sent the letter.'

Watson
What about the missing shoes?

Holmes
Elementary, dear Watson. He needed something to give the starving hound Sir Henry's scent, so he paid a maid at Sir Henry's hotel to steal one of his shoes. The first one was a new one, and didn't have Sir Henry's scent on it. It was no use for the hound, so another, older, shoe was stolen. With that, I knew that the hound must be a natural and not a supernatural creature.'

Watson
So by the time I arrived here in Devonshire, you knew that there was a real hound, and that we were looking for a man and a woman.

Holmes
I guessed that the Stapletons were the pair. I had to watch Stapleton, but I had to hide myself. As I have explained, I could not tell you what I was doing. I stayed in Newtown and used the hut on the moor only when necessary. Your letters were brought to me immediately from Baker Street—

Watson
The boy...one of your Irregulars, I presume.

Holmes
When you told me that Stapleton had owned a school in the north of England, I checked on him and where he had come from. I discovered he had come from South America. And then everything became clear.

Watson
You knew everything.

Holmes
But I could prove nothing. We had to catch the man doing something criminal, and so I had to put Sir Henry in danger.'

Stapleton
You're as monstrous as I am. You let a man die to solve your precious mystery!

Holmes (smiling, looking down at Henry)
Yes, I must apologize to you, Sir Henry. I put your life in danger. I expected to see a huge hound, but not a creature like that. The fog gave us a very short time to control our fear, and for moments we could not move.

(Henry jumps up, revealing that he is not hurt in the least)

Henry
Never mind. You saved my life, and I thank you.

Miss Stapleton
You're alive! Oh, thank God.

Watson
All part of the plan? (nodding) Of course, he could not frighten Sir Henry in the same way as Sir Charles. Sir Henry is a young and healthy man. So he kept the hound hungry. He knew that the animal would either kill Sir Henry or would hurt him so badly that it would be easy to complete the murder.

Holmes
But not tonight. His heart may be sad, but it is not weak. Sir Henry will take some time to get over the lovely Miss Stapleton. The truth is often complicated. Love...as they say...hurts.

Miss Stapleton
I wanted to help you...to love you...but it's impossible.

Holmes
Touching. (unphased) What do you say, Stapleton? Clever, yet stupid. Living so close to Baskerville Hall and using a false name...it looks very strange. How would you have explained that to the police, if after Sir Henry's death you inherited the Baskerville lands and fortune? How had you planned to explain the false name and why you were living at Pen House? Had you thought of an answer to that problem?

(All are silent. Sound effect of Police arriving)

Holmes
'But that's enough work for the evening, Watson. The police have arrived. I have two tickets, for the theatre. If we get out now, we shall make the last train and have time to stop at my favorite restaurant for some dinner on the way.'

END of SCENE

The End

Cast Bows.

www.ingramcontent.com/pod-product-compliance
Ingram Content Group UK Ltd.
Pitfield, Milton Keynes, MK11 3LW, UK
UKHW020216250726
13967UKWH00001B/34

9 781312 080133